A Life of Significance with Jesus

SERIES

Knowing What
Christians
Believe

wesleyan
publishing
house

Indianapolis, Indiana

Copyright © 2007 by Wesleyan Publishing House
Published by Wesleyan Publishing House
Indianapolis, Indiana 46250
Printed in the United States of America

ISBN: 978-0-89827-367-0

Written by Andrea Summers.

Cover design by Kory Pence.

All Scripture quotations, unless otherwise indicated, are taken from the
HOLY BIBLE, NEW INTERNATIONAL VERSION ®. NIV ®. Copyright 1973, 1978,
1984 by the International Bible Society. Used by permission of Zondervan.
All rights reserved.

All rights reserved. No part of this publication may be reproduced, stored
in a retrieval system, or transmitted in any form or by any means—elec-
tronic, mechanical, photocopy, recording or any other—except for brief
quotations in printed reviews, without the prior written permission of the
publisher.

D-SERIES

A Life of Significance with Jesus

Everyone wants their life to count for something significant. People everywhere are spending their lives for fading artifacts and fleeting glory. Significance, value, legacy, and impact are the desired outcome of every investment. The desire of believers in Jesus Christ should be no different. Those who are true followers of Jesus Christ are to be interested in becoming more and more like Him. Following Jesus and getting closer to Him *IS* significance, value, legacy, and impact for a Christian.

The *D Series* works by connecting every person to a solid relationship with Jesus. The scope of what we can learn and live for Jesus is limitless. But this series will get every believer on the right path—no matter where your starting point is. Regardless if you are a new believer or a seasoned disciple, this series is filled with truth for every person in the local Church.

What is significant about the *D Series* is the expectation that participants will actually live what they are studying. It is not enough to fill our heads and hearts with Jesus. We must follow through and make sure His love and interest in others show up in our service and daily activity. In other words, Christlike, holy living results when we use our heads, hearts, hands, and habits to focus on and represent Jesus.

Give yourself, your time, and your focus to Jesus through the *D Series*. Live your beliefs out in Jesus everyday!

THE COMMUNITY OF SPIRITUAL FORMATION

To illustrate it simply, there are four areas to engage: the head, heart, hands, and habits. Start by seeking knowledge and understanding of Jesus Christ. This wisdom will enter your heart and miraculously transform it. A unified heart and mind leads to a wholehearted expression of love through compassionate service. This outpouring of compassion becomes a daily way of life where we are given daily grace by God's Holy Spirit to live a holy life.

Coming full circle—your growing wisdom, unified heart, compassionate service, and daily holy living—you are driven to a community of spiritual formation where every believer looks more and more like Jesus. The result is a solid relationship with Jesus and a lasting significance, value, legacy, and impact in the lives of those we serve.

Dr. Jim Dunn
General Director
Spiritual Formation Department
The Wesleyan Church

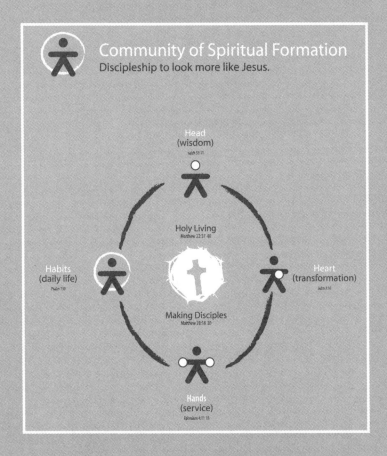

Community of Spiritual Formation
Discipleship to look more like Jesus.

Contents

Introduction

Imagine a big glass jar and a neat pile of rocks sitting in front of you, along with a great big bag of sand. Imagine, also, that your task is to fit all the rocks into the big glass jar. It does not matter how much sand fits into the jar as long as all the rocks are in and the jar is completely full. What should your strategy be? Should you start with the rocks or the sand?

It doesn't take a genius to figure out that if you start out by filling the jar with sand, you won't have room for any rocks. But that if you fill the jar with rocks first and then pack the sand in around the rocks you will have accomplished your task.

Filling a jar by putting the biggest stuff in first just makes sense. Likewise, it just makes sense to have a strong foundation for your Christian beliefs. Some of the basics, or "rocks," of your faith are centered around God, Jesus, the Bible, and Christian living. In fact, what you believe about these "rocks" influences every facet of faith and life. So it is important to make sure you have these core pieces of Christian faith "in the jar." And it is not just about making sure you believe the right stuff, but those right beliefs inform the way you live each day.

Over the next several weeks you will learn foundational truths about your faith and be challenged to live life in light of these basic beliefs.

What Is God Like?

JEREMIAH 32:17

INTRODUCTION

From looking at a snapshot of someone, you can perhaps tell their approximate height, what color their hair is, or whether they have dimples. But that snapshot would reveal very little about the person's hopes, dreams, and loves, not to mention their favorite ice cream flavor. Likewise, any description of God is barely even a snapshot. Human language is simply incapable of depicting God's immenseness.

But, Christians cannot stay silent. While He is veiled in mystery, He has also revealed himself through creation and Scripture. He has revealed himself powerfully through Christ. Our knowledge of God, though not exhaustive, is genuine. Let's take a look at some important attributes of God, asking the question, "What is God like?"

ICEBREAKER

What are some common misconceptions about God evident in our culture? In the Church?

From the misconceptions about God listed below, which one do you most often find yourself slipping into?

- Heavenly Grandfather—loving, forgetful grandfather who helps us out if we ask loudly enough

- Santa Claus—gives away the "good things of life" if we are well-behaved

- Heavenly Handyman—steps in to fix life when it is breaks down

- Judge—ready to condemn those who don't stay on His good side

- The Force—impersonable, unknowable force in the universe

Our words and thoughts are leaky buckets when it comes to describing God.

—Moore

Nature is an unlimited broadcasting station, through which God speaks to us every hour, if we only will tune in.

—George Washington Carver

DISCOVERING TRUTH—HEAD

What is God like, anyway? Answers to this question can vary greatly because our understanding of God is limited and influenced by upbringing, media, biases, and ignorance. Many mistaken ideas about God show up in our thoughts, in conversations with others, and in the church. The fact is that God exists far beyond our capacity to understand or define Him. He is infinite, and our minds are finite.

However, everything we need to know about God has been revealed in Scripture. In fact, the Bible is filled with descriptions of the characteristics God. Here are a few key attributes of God found in Scripture:

The universe is but one vast Symbol of God.

—Thomas Carlyle

1. God is power—God has the ability to do anything consistent with His nature. God's power is immeasurable. The picture of power that our wildest imaginations can conjure is a drop in the bucket compared to God's power.

Have someone read Jeremiah 32:17 aloud.

Jeremiah offers the heavens and the earth as examples of God's power. What other examples of God's power can you think of?

Why might it be important to qualify God's power by specifying that He can do anything "consistent with his nature"?

2. God is holy—God is completely pure, and no evil whatsoever resides in His character. Just as it is impossible to be "mostly pregnant," it is also

impossible to be "mostly holy." You are either pregnant or you're not; there are no degrees of pregnant-ness. Likewise, God is completely pure, unable to tolerate sin.

Have someone read Psalm 18:30.

Describe what you think of when you hear the word *pure.*

3. God is love—Love is not just something God does, it is who God is. Love is His very nature. Our existence and our redemption are all motivated by God's love.

Have someone read 1 John 4:8–10. Have someone else read John 3:16–17.

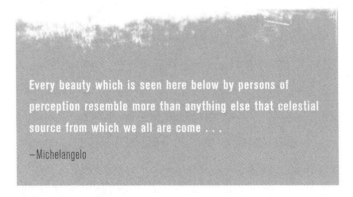

Every beauty which is seen here below by persons of perception resemble more than anything else that celestial source from which we all are come . . .

—Michelangelo

Love, in 1 John, is defined in light of God's love not ours. List some ways God's love is different from our love.

The Bible also gives us pictures of God's justice, mercy, righteousness, truth, and grace, to name a few. And although words can never adequately describe God, these biblical concepts give us a black-and-white glimpse of this awesome, full-color God!

EMBRACING TRUTH—HEART

With a blank piece of paper and a pencil, take three to five minutes to draw a picture of God without using any words. When everyone is finished, share your "artwork" with each other. What attributes of God are inherent in each other's artwork?

Divide up into groups of two or three and share a time when God made His love particularly evident to you.

This session's list of attributes of God was anything but exhaustive. Using a whiteboard, list some important attributes of God not mentioned in the session.

Which attribute of God particularly stuck out to you today and why? Is it an attribute of God that you consider often or hardly at all? Take turns sharing your thoughts with the group.

CONNECTING—HANDS

Praise is a natural response to God and His attributes. If someone in your group plays guitar and/or can facilitate worship, take turns suggesting hymns or choruses that highlight attributes of God discussed in the session, and then sing them together.

God calls us to be like Him in His attribute of love. Who, in your life, do you need to love unconditionally? Ask God to fill you with His love, remembering that this love is not something God does but it is who God is.

TAKE HOME—HABITS

The knowledge of who God is changes the way we live. In light of God's power, is there doubt, worry, or fear that you need to surrender to God?

In light of God's holiness, is there sin or impurity you need to confess to God?

In light of God's love for you is there low self-esteem that you need to release? Or is there ill-will toward another person that you need to confess and replace with God's love?

LOOKING FORWARD

Who is Jesus? And what boldness motivates Him to claim that He is the only way to the Father? Have you ever wondered why Jesus has the corner on the market in terms of salvation?

DIG DEEPER

1. A.W. Tozer wrote, "What comes into our minds when we think about God is the most important thing about us." What is it that comes into your mind when you think about God? Over the next five days, fill your mind with Scripture that tells us who God is, studying a different attribute each day: **Day 1**: Wise—Romans 11:33. **Day 2**: Immortal,

Infinite—Deuteronomy 33:27; Psalm 90:2; 1 Timothy 1:17. **Day 3**: Trustworthy—Malachi 3:6; Numbers 23:19; Psalm 102:26–27. **Day 4**: Unfathomable, beyond our understanding—Isaiah 40:28; Psalm 145:3; Romans 11:33–34. **Day 5**: God is one—Deuteronomy 6:4.

2. Read together through these names of God and the corresponding verses that help us understand what God is like: *Elohim*—strong one, divine (Gen. 1:1). *Adonai*—Lord, indicating a Master to servant relationship (Ex. 4:10, 13). *El Elyon*—Most High, the strongest one (Gen. 14:20). *El Roi*—the strong one who sees (Gen. 16:13). *El Shaddai*—Almighty God (Gen. 17:1). *El Olam*—everlasting God (Isa. 40:28). *Yahweh*—Lord "I Am," meaning the eternal self-existent God (Ex. 3:13–14).

3. Read Deuteronomy 4:35–40, in which the Israelites were encouraged to remember God's faithfulness. Then spend some time remembering (pray, journal, etc.) the ways God has worked in your life and proven himself faithful.

DISCOVERING TRUTH – HEAD

Divide into groups of two and go to a crowded place like the mall or a college campus. Then begin "interviewing" people you run into by asking, "What is God like?" Record the answers you receive by either videotaping or by writing them down.

EMBRACING TRUTH – HEART

God reveals himself to us through a variety of ways, including Scripture and nature. Incorporate these by planning a day-hike as a group. As you hike together, ask God to reveal himself to you through nature. Halfway through the hike find a place to spread out and meditate on Deuteronomy 4:35–40. Ask God to reveal himself to you through this Scripture. When your group has completed the hike sit down together and reflect aloud how God revealed himself to each of you individually. You may find that God will reveal himself to you, not just through nature and Scripture, but through some of your group members as well.

CONNECTING - HANDS

A great resource for learning more about who God is, *Knowing God* by J. I. Packer.

NOTES:
HEAD, HEART, HANDS & HABITS

Who is Jesus?

JOHN 14:6

INTRODUCTION

William Tyndale, an English Bible translator, could not find an English word that adequately described what Jesus did for us on the cross. So, he made up a word by combining "at" and "onement." Jesus is the atonement for our sins, bringing sinful humanity together with God. Jesus is the bridge that covers the gap left by sin between God and humanity, and it is impossible for God and humanity to be one without Jesus.

Jesus told His disciples, "I am the way and the truth and the life. No one comes to the Father except through me" (John 14:6). He did not merely point the way to God. He himself claimed to be the only way to the Father and the source of eternal truth and life.

Let's take a look at Jesus' claim to be the only way of salvation and shed some light on who Jesus is.

ICEBREAKER

"As long as you believe in God and try to be a good person, it doesn't matter what religion you belong to." Have you ever heard a statement like this? It seems tolerant, reasonable, and politically correct. But Jesus said it's wrong. What are some other statements like this you have encountered?

Why is the idea that Jesus is the *only* way to the Father so difficult for people to swallow?

DISCOVERING TRUTH—HEAD

Because of sin, the way to heaven is closed, and it is not God who put up the roadblock, but us. Only God can remove the roadblock and open the way. But Jesus is more than a spiritual guide showing us the way we ought to walk. Jesus is the path and the way. Jesus spans the distance between God and us. Because of our sin, we

Jesus tapped me on the shoulder and said, "Bob, why are you resisting me?" I said, I'm not resisting you! He said, "You gonna follow me?" I said, I've never thought about that before! He said, "When you're not following me, you're resisting me." —Bob Dylan

cannot get to God. But God came to us in the person of Jesus.

But to understand why Jesus called himself the way, we need to take a quick look at the Old Testament. In the Old Testament people brought animal sacrifices to God each year to demonstrate their sorrow for sins. And the sacrificial animals had to be the best animals—without blemish, perfect. The animals symbolically took on the sins of the people and then died for those sins. People repeated this ritual year after year.

Jesus, however, fulfilled the Old Testament sacrificial system with His death on the cross. Taking on the sins of all humanity, Jesus died for those sins. Christ's sacrifice is perfect and complete, and no other sacrifice is ever needed.

The knowledge of God without that of man's misery causes pride. The knowledge of man's misery without that of God causes despair. The knowledge of Jesus Christ constitutes the middle course, because in Him we find both God and our misery. —Blaise Pascal

Have someone read 1 John 2:2 and Ephesians 1:7–8.

What does Jesus' sacrifice on the cross accomplish that the old sacrificial system could not?

Jesus not only claimed He was the way, but the truth as well. Without Christ, we are under the power of the evil one and subject to his lies and deceit. But through Christ, God's truth becomes a reality in our lives. However, Jesus is more than a great spiritual teacher who uncovers doctrine about God. Jesus is, himself, the truth about God. He is the complete and final revelation of who God is. Ultimate truth is found in the person of Jesus Christ. He reveals God and exposes us.

Have someone read Colossians 2:3.

What do you think the statement "all truth is God's truth" might mean in light of John 14:6 and Colossians 2:3?

Finally, Christ not only claimed to be the way and the truth, but the life as well. We are spiritually lifeless without Christ. But Jesus is more than a spiritual doctor who diagnoses us and makes us feel better. Jesus is life itself, and it is through Him that we are freed from death. He gives us not only commandments and noble ideals, but also the power to live them out, the power to become new people.

The dearest friend on earth is a mere shadow compared to Jesus Christ. —Oswald Chambers

In Jesus, God wills to be true God not only in the height but also in the depth—in the depth of human creatureliness, sinfulness and mortality. —Karl Barth

Have someone read John 10:7–10.

What do you think "life to the full" in Christ looks like?

In John 14:6, Jesus added, "No one comes to the Father except through me." Christ is the only way to God. It is utterly impossible to win God's favor by any efforts of our own.

EMBRACING TRUTH—HEART

While you may know that it is impossible to win God's favor by your own efforts, it is human nature to try to "do things" and "be better" in our own strength. Where do you see that showing up in your own life? Where are you tempted to do it yourself?

Take some time to journal about one of the following ideas. Write about a time in your life when you experienced forgiveness from sin. Or, if you have never experienced forgiveness from sin, write a letter to God expressing your desire (or perhaps even lack thereof) for forgiveness.

Reread John 3:16. The word often translated "one and only" ("he gave his *only* begotten Son" [King James Version]) can also be translated "unique." The author is not trying to say that Jesus is God's only son, but emphasizing that Jesus is God's "one of a kind" Son with significantly unique attributes and purpose. Using a whiteboard, brainstorm, as a group, what is significantly unique about Christ.

CONNECTING—HANDS

Do the people you live life with know your spiritual story (testimony)? Do you know theirs? Plan to share your testimony with someone this week, and/or plan to ask someone else to share his or her testimony with you this week.

Jesus said that He is the way, the truth and the life. Think of someone who is living life to the full (see John 10:7–10 again) and articulate to the person next to you why you thought of that person. In terms of living life to the full, what would others say about you? Would others think of you as an example of this encouragement?

TAKE HOME—HABITS

Jesus said that He is the *way*, the truth, and the life. How should you live differently in light of this reality? For example, have you made a decision for Christ? Do you care about the eternal destiny of others? Do you have freedom from the guilt of sin?

Do you have doubts about Jesus' claim to be the only way to the Father? If so, do not be afraid to talk to someone you respect, pray about your doubt, or read up on the issue.

LOOKING FORWARD

Do you feel like reading the Bible is (A) like reading the rules posted next to the swimming pool, (B) like reading an electro-physics textbook, or (C) like reading the instruction manual for virtually any toy that requires assembly? Next week, find out what is so special about the Bible.

DIG DEEPER

1. Who is Jesus?
   Read what the disciples said about Him
   (Mark 4:4).

   Read what the crowds said about Him
   (Luke 9:18–19).

   Read what the apostle Paul said about Him
   (Colossians 1:15–16).

   Try articulating in one or two sentences
   who you believe Jesus is.

2. The following are quotes about Jesus
   from church fathers who all lived during
   the first 500 years after Christ's death and
   resurrection. Read these words about
   Jesus and choose one that sticks out to
   you the most. Then search for more writ-
   ings by that person (either online or in a
   library) and do some more reading about
   Jesus.

   God has revealed himself in his Son Jesus
   Christ, who is his Word issuing from the
   silence.

   —St. Ignatius of Antioch (died 110)

Jesus whom I know as my Redeemer cannot be less than God.

—St. Athanasius (296–373).

Christ is the great hidden mystery, the blessed goal, the purpose for which everything was created.

—St. Maximus the Confessor, Byzantine theologian (580–662)

3. Read through the book of Mark and underline each occurrence of the word compassion. Then look up its meaning online or in a dictionary. Jesus' ministry operated out of compassion for humanity.

DISCOVERING TRUTH - HEAD

The Apostles' Creed, written in the sixth or seventh century, was a baptismal creed for new Christians. It encapsulated the core beliefs of the faith then and still does so today. Read through the Apostles' Creed together.

EMBRACING TRUTH - HEART

Divide into groups of two and go to a crowded place like the mall or a college campus. Then begin "interviewing" people you run into by asking, "Who is Jesus?" Record the answers you receive by either videotaping or by writing them down.

CONNECTING - HANDS

Hook up a laptop (with Internet access) to a projector and experience together the visual presentations of the last words of Jesus found at: http://www.rejesus.co.uk/spirituality/seven_sayings/index.html#

What's So Special about the Bible?

2 TIMOTHY 3:15-17

INTRODUCTION

The Bible is the authority for the faith and practice of Christians. In Herbert Workman's *Persecution in the Early Church*, the implications of scriptural authority are evident in the life of a North African bishop. In A.D. 303, when it was still illegal to be a Christian, the Roman emperor Diocletian issued a decree that he hoped would keep Christianity from spreading. The main objective of the decree was the destruction of the Christian Scriptures. A man named Felix was the bishop of a village near Carthage when the mayor of the town ordered him to hand over his Scriptures. Felix refused to surrender the Word of God, and so he was finally shipped to Italy, where he was martyred rather than surrender his Gospels.

With multiple Bibles on our bookshelves, it is hard to relate to Felix's resolve. What is so special about the Bible that it would compel Felix to sacrifice his life? Certainly, Felix understood something about the great importance of the Scriptures.

ICEBREAKER

Pictionary: Bible style. Divide into two teams and take turns pulling names of Bible characters out of a hat and drawing them for your team. If, after one minute, your team has been unsuccessful, then the character's name is passed to the other team, who is given thirty seconds to guess. After three rounds or so (depending on the size of your group), the team with the most correct guesses in the allotted time period wins. Have one person who is willing to sit out come up with the Bible character names and write them on slips of paper. Some examples of biblical characters that can be used are Abraham, Samson, Ruth, and Peter.

> The Bible . . . banned, burned, beloved. More widely read, more frequently attacked than any other book in history. Generations of intellectuals have attempted to discredit it, dictators of every age have outlawed it and executed those who read it. Yet soldiers carry it into battle believing it more powerful than their weapons. Fragments of it smuggled into solitary prison cells have transformed ruthless killers into gentle saints. —Charles Colson

DISCOVERING TRUTH—HEAD

Christianity is inextricably linked to the Bible. God decided to communicate to men and women in a way that they could understand—through human history. The Scriptures are more than a record of God's words, they are the Word of God. They not only contain an account of God's acts, but the Scriptures are also able to act on the hearts of men and women and bring about life change. The theme running through the sixty-six books is the story of human rebellion against God and His merciful acts intended to bring about repentance and faith in men and women.

The highest earthly enjoyments are but a shadow of the joy I find in reading God's Word. —Lady Jane Grey

The Bible redirects my will, cleanses my emotions, enlightens my mind, and quickens my total being.

—E. Stanley Jones

The Bible came about by ordinary means as people wrote the words. However, the Bible contains a divine message given to writers in supernatural ways. The Holy Spirit guided the Biblical authors in their thoughts and words, and the Holy Spirit has kept errors of essential doctrine out of Scripture.

Have someone read 2 Peter 1:20–21.

Peter used prophecy (he is referring to Old Testament Scriptures) to substantiate his claim that Jesus Christ is the divine son of God (see verses 16–18). Revealing Jesus' identity is an important purpose of all Scripture. The authority of Scripture is a question about who is responsible for the words. To whom does 2 Peter 1:20–21 attribute the origin of Scripture?

Have someone read 2 Timothy 3:15–17.

"God-breathed" is a Hebrew way of saying that something was produced by the power or the energy of God. Scripture came to writers as a result of God's initiative, not human initiative. Therefore, the Bible is both divine and human: It is both the Word of God and the words of the writers.

If the books of the Bible are inspired by God and simultaneously retain the unique style and perspective of its authors, how does this affect the way we study, interpret, and apply its truths?

The Bible is, according to 2 Timothy 3:15–17, "useful." For what is it useful, and where do you see this usefulness in your life?

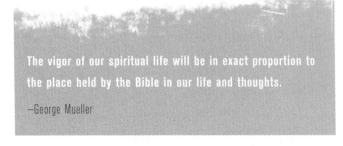

The vigor of our spiritual life will be in exact proportion to the place held by the Bible in our life and thoughts.

–George Mueller

EMBRACING TRUTH—HEART

Second Timothy uses the word "useful" to describe Scripture. What do you think of when you hear the word *useful*? In your group, shout out the first couple things that come to mind. How often do you rely on these things? Weekly? Daily? Hourly?

Read Mark 4:1–8, first praying for the Holy Spirit's illumination and for life transformation. Read through the passage three times, the first time asking, "What was Jesus trying to communicate to His listeners?" The second time, ask, "What was the author, Mark, trying to communicate to his readers?" The third time, ask, "What is God trying to say to me, today?"

Journal about one or two roadblocks that may keep you from reading God's Word and applying it to your life.

CONNECTING—HANDS

Divide into groups of two or three and discuss your study and application of Mark 4:1–8. As you do this, observe the different applications to the same Scripture. This is evidence of the Holy Spirit!

Has your Bible learning been in community or alone? Remember that a balance of Bible learning in a group and alone is necessary for healthy spiritual growth.

TAKE HOME—HABITS

The Bible is so much more than a "book." Its also a tool for spiritual transformation. This will look different for each person.

Be intentional about studying Scripture in the context of community. Brainstorm as a group ways that this can be accomplished (for example, being intentional about discussing the sermon at lunch after church).

LOOKING FORWARD

According to Dan Kimball, people's number three fear (behind public speaking and death) is evangelical Christians. If believers are called to be salt and light in the world, why is it that the world is afraid of us? Next week, learn more about the Bible's mandate for believers to have a transforming effect on the world.

DIG DEEPER

1. Scripture is often referred to as God speaking. While God's word includes more than Scripture (i.e. nature, proclamation, etc.), Scripture is a very significant way that God communicates with us. Take a look at the following verses that either directly or indirectly attribute the origin of Scripture to God: Romans 9:17 *and* Exodus 9:16; Galatians 3:8 *and* Genesis 12:3.

2. The Holy Spirit reveals truth in Scripture to us. Read 1 Corinthians 1:12–13. What does it say about the Holy Spirit's role in revelation?

3. Read the books of Mark and John. They are both accounts of Christ's life and are both inspired (God-breathed) Scripture. Yet, they both reflect the individual styles, purposes, and experiences of their authors. As you read these books, take note of these differences.

DISCOVERING TRUTH – HEAD

Have someone read 1 Thessalonians 2:13. While Paul is not talking about Scripture here, it is a great example of the way that God speaks in and through the words of people. Take turns sharing a time in your life when God used someone's words (in Scripture or through another person) to speak to you.

EMBRACING TRUTH – HEART

Why is it that though we own and revere the Word of God, we don't always read and feed upon it as we should? Have someone read Hebrews 4:12. What keeps you from reading and living out God's Word? Is the Bible too familiar? Is it too foreign? Is it too powerful?

OPTIONAL LEARNING ACTIVITY 3:
CONNECTING - HANDS

Chances are you learned Scripture from others. And we are more inclined to hear truth from Scripture when we can see the wisdom, power, and authority of God in their lives. Take turns naming someone who has influenced you by living out the Scriptures. Also name someone you would like to similarly influence (children, spouse, co-worker).

NOTES:
HEAD, HEART, HANDS & HABITS

Transforming Effect

MATTHEW 5:13-16

INTRODUCTION

Imagine that you fight fires for a living. It is your responsibility to put out fires, and if there is ever a fire in your community you play a key role in protecting innocent people by putting out those fires. Fortunately, fighting the fires in your community doesn't consume all your time. And so, you have the task of washing the truck in-between fires. Other people in your small group have the task of cooking, cleaning the firehouse, and maintaining the equipment.

Now, to make sure you understand your responsibility, fill in the blank: What is your job? _____

You may have been tempted to say that your job is washing the truck. But, I'm sure you're catching on by now that washing the truck is not your job. You fight fires. You may have other tasks to do, but your job is fighting fires.

Many Christians have the same problem. Our job is to be salt and light and to share God's love with others. You may have other tasks like being a teacher, an accountant, a mother, or even a pastor. But your primary duty is to bring others to Christ.

ICEBREAKER

As a group, brainstorm and then agree upon the top three mistakes Christians make when they witness. Get a few volunteers to act out these witnessing *faux pas.*

DISCOVERING TRUTH—HEAD

In the Sermon on the Mount, Jesus explained what is expected of believers in the world: they are to function like salt and like light. Salt has some useful properties. First, it acts as a preservative for rotting meat. Where there is no refrigeration, people rub salt into meat to keep

Where'er a noble deed is wrought,
where'er is spoken a noble thought,
our hearts in glad surprise
to high levels rise.

—Henry Wadsworth Longfellow

it from going bad. Second, salt is necessary for flavor, adding taste to food.

Have someone read Matthew 5:13.

What are the implications of acting as a preservative in the world? How are Christians to add flavor to the world?

Jesus went on to explain that believers are not only to function as salt, but also as light in the world as well. Light eradicates darkness and it makes it possible to see.

Have someone read Matthew 5:14–15.

> **When you see your brother, you see God.**
>
> –St. Clement of Alexandria
>
> **Love is doing small things with great love.**
>
> –Mother Teresa

What are the implications of acting as light in the world? What does it mean to eradicate darkness and make it possible for others to see?

We are to be like a city on a hill and a candle on a stand— we are to shine. What is this light that we exude? Jesus said that we are to let our light shine, not so that people can see us, but so that people can see our good works and praise God. The light we are to shine is the moral and spiritual goodness of our lives lived out in a dark world. We teach others about God with the character and shape of our lives. Our faith lived out in goodness points others to God! But this usefulness is not a given! Salt can lose its "saltiness" and light can be hidden under a bowl. We are to be in the world, but different from the world. If we are Christians, shining is our business in the world.

Have someone read Matthew 5:16.

Jesus suggested that our good deeds do not go unnoticed by the world, but instead cause some to praise Him. How would you define good deeds? What do they look like? Where does their motivation come from?

EMBRACING TRUTH—HEART

Using a white board, make two columns with these headings: "tasty" and "bland." Then, as a group, brainstorm qualities of "tasty" Christians (believers who are living as

All the kindness which a man puts out into the world works on the hearts and thoughts of mankind.

–Albert Schweitzer

There is a God-shaped vacuum in the heart of every man which cannot be filled by any created thing, but only by God, the Creator, made known through Jesus.

–Blaise Pascal

salt in the world) and "bland" Christians (those who claim Christ but have lost their saltiness).

In Matthew 5:13–15 Jesus described salt as useful. How are believers to be useful salt and light in the world? Are you useful? Are you allowing God to use you?

Salt and light are meant to be a part of the world, and yet distinctively different from the world. But too many Christians look exactly like the world. And some Christians are so out of touch with the world they have become irrelevant. Discuss what a balance should look like. Then take a few minutes to journal about what this balance should look like in your own life.

CONNECTING—HANDS

Identify two people in your life to whom you need to be salt and light. Divide into groups of two and pray for these people specifically and by name.

Matthew 5:16 says, "Let your light shine before men, that they may see your good deeds and praise your Father in heaven." These good deeds are not about what you do, but about who you are. However, deeds imply action of some kind. So, think outside the box . . . what are some good deeds you can live out?

TAKE HOME—HABITS

Salt is useful because it preserves and adds flavor. Light is useful because it gets rid of darkness. Of these particular "uses," which do you identify with most readily? What can you do to be tastier or preserve better, or shine more brightly?

Think of the two people you identified in the previous section. What is one first step you can make toward being salt and light to these people?

Have a poster board handy, and have each person write their two names on it. Put this poster board in a prominent place where it will be seen by the entire group.

LOOKING FORWARD

Church rituals like communion and baptism are a means
of grace for believers. They serve to grow us toward God
and toward each other as well. In the next volume you
will learn more about these important sacraments of the
Church.

DIG DEEPER

1. Read Matthew 5:13–16 again. Salt is a hidden but powerful influence. Light is a visible and revealing influence. Think of an example of a believer's hidden but powerful influence in the world. Then think of an example of a believer's visible and revealing influence in the world.

2. Read Matthew 5:10 and Matthew 5:12. These verses precede the passage of study in this session. Jesus shared them all as a part of His Sermon on the Mount. Jesus promised that those who have the character of God can expect persecution and rejection. So, a by-product of being salt and light is persecution and rejection. How does this make you feel? How should you respond to persecution when it comes your way? According to Matthew 5:12, why are we to rejoice when we are persecuted?

3. Read the following passages that mention salt: Leviticus 2:13; Ezra 6:9; Ezekiel 43:24; Numbers 18:19; Job 6:6; Colossians 4:6. How do these biblical references to salt inform Jesus' mention of salt in Matthew 5?

DISCOVERING TRUTH - HEAD

Martyn Lloyd-Jones wrote, "Most competent historians are agreed in saying that what undoubtedly saved [England] from a revolution such as that experienced in France at the end of the eighteenth century was nothing but the Evangelical Revival. This was not because anything was done directly, but because masses of individuals had become Christians and were living this better life and had this higher outlook. The whole political situation was affected, and the great Acts of Parliament which were passed in the last century were mostly due to the fact that there were such large numbers of Christians found in the land." One important Act of Parliament that was passed was the abolition of slavery in England. When you look at our culture and our world today, what preserving (salty) influence should the Church have on the world? Discuss this as a group.

EMBRACING TRUTH - HEART

Have three group members practice and present this reader's theater piece to the group.

READER 1: Blessed are you when people insult you,

READER 2: Insult you

READER 3: persecute you

READER 1: Attack you

READER 2: and falsely say all kinds of evil against you because of me.

READER 3: Tell lies about you

READER 1: Slander you

READER 2: All because of your association with Jesus

READER 3: Because of Jesus

ALL: Rejoice and be glad,

READER 1: Yes, rejoice,

READER 2: because great is your reward in heaven,

READER 3: for in the same way they persecuted the prophets who were before you.

READER 1: You are the salt of the earth.

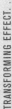

TRANSFORMING EFFECT.

READER 2: Salt of the earth

READER 3: Salt for the world

READER 1: But if the salt loses its saltiness,

READER 2: Its tang,

READER 3: Its distinctive flavor

READER 1: how can it be made salty again?

READER 2: It is no longer good for anything,

READER 3: It's worthless

READER 1: except to be thrown out and trampled by men.

READER 2: Trampled

[pause]

READER 1: You are the light of the world.

READER 2: You are salt

READER 3: You are light

READER 1: You are the light of the world.

READER 2: Light FOR the world

READER 1: A city on a hill cannot be hidden.

READER 2: You can see it from afar off.

READER 1: Neither do people light a lamp and put it under
a bowl.

READER 2: Instead they put it on its stand,

READER 3: High up

READER 2: In the open

READER 3: and it gives light to everyone in the house.

READER 1: You don't hide a city

READER 2: You don't hide a light

READER 3: Only people who are afraid hide their light

READER 1: Let it shine

ALL: Let it shine

READER 1: Let your light shine before men,

READER 2: Before men and women

READER 3: Before your friends and associates

READER 1: Before your school friends

READER 2: And work friends

READER 3: And neighbors

READER 2: And relatives

READER 3: Yes, relatives

READER 2: How about enemies?

READER 3: Yes, let it shine before your enemies, too

READER 1: Let your light shine before men, that they may see your good deeds

READER 2: Your character

READER 3: Your love

READER 1: Your unselfishness

READER 2: Your compassion and kindness

READER 3: Your good deeds

READER 1: Let your light shine before men, that they may see your good deeds and praise your Father in heaven.

READER 2: Praise your Father

READER 3: Your light prompts praise

READER 1: Your saltiness elicits worship

READER 2: Of your Father

READER 3: Of their Father

READER 1: To the glory of God

READER 2: To His glory

ALL: To His glory!

READER 1: Let your light shine before men, that they may see your good deeds and praise your Father in heaven.

(Source: http://www.jesuswalk.com/manifesto/rt-salt-light.htm)

OPTIONAL LEARNING ACTIVITY 3:
CONNECTING - HANDS

Discuss the often quoted question, "If you were on trial for being a Christian, would there be enough evidence to convict you?" First, talk about what constitutes "evidence" for authentic faith. Second, discuss where this "evidence" shows up in your own lives.

NOTES:
HEAD, HEART, HANDS & HABITS

NOTES:
HEAD, HEART, HANDS & HABITS